Guidelines for Leading Your Congregation

CHILDREN'S MINISTRIES
Ministries that help children grow in faith

By Mary Alice Gran
General Board of Discipleship

CHILDREN'S MINISTRIES

Copyright © 2004 by Cokesbury

All rights reserved.
United Methodist churches and other official United Methodist bodies may reproduce up to 500 words from this publication, provided the following notice appears with the excerpted material: From *Children's Ministries: 2005–2008*. Copyright © 2004 by Cokesbury. Used by permission.

Requests for quotations exceeding 500 words should be addressed to Permissions Office, Abingdon Press, P.O. Box 801, 201 Eighth Avenue South, Nashville, TN 37202-0801 or permissions@abingdonpress.com.

This book is printed on acid-free paper.

ISBN 0-687-00260-5

All Scripture quotations unless noted otherwise are taken from the *New Revised Standard Version of the Bible,* copyright 1989, by the Division of Christian Education of the National Council of the Churches of Christ in the United States of America. Used by permission. All rights reserved.

MANUFACTURED IN THE UNITED STATES OF AMERICA

CONTENTS

Our Identity, Call, and Mission **4**

Welcome to Children's Ministries **6**
    A Biblical Foundation

Getting Started **8**
    What Is My Job?
    Basic Responsibilities
    The Coordinator of Children's Ministries
    Quick-Start Tips

Keeping Our Commitments to Children **13**
    The United Methodist Church
    Your Commitment
    The Congregation's Commitment
    Children's Ministry Profile

What Is Your Role in Keeping Children Safe? **18**

Children in the Life of the Congregation **19**
    Gifts Children Bring to the Church

The Organizational Structure of the Church **21**
    Congregational Meeting Commitment Worksheet
    How to Form a Council on Children's Ministries

Ministry for, with, and by Children **24**

Ministry in the Community and the World **27**

Organize and Plan for the Year **30**

Weekday Ministries **31**
    What Is Weekday Ministry?
    Weekday Ministry Programs

Resources **35**

General Agency Contacts .... **Inside Back Cover**

Our Identity, Call, and Mission

You are so important to the life of the Christian church! You have consented to be among a great and long line of people who have shared the faith and led others in the work of Jesus Christ. We have the church only because over the millennia people like you have caught the vision of God's kingdom and have claimed a place in the faith community to extend God's love to others. You have been called and have committed your unique passions, gifts, and abilities in a position of leadership, and this guide will help you understand some of the elements of that ministry and how it fits within the mission of your church and of The United Methodist Church.

"The mission of the Church is to make disciples of Jesus Christ. Local churches provide the most significant arena through which disciple-making occurs" (*The Book of Discipline of The United Methodist Church, 2004,* ¶120). The church is not only local but also global, and it is for everyone. Our church has an organizational structure through which we work, but it is a living organism as well. Each person is called to ministry by virtue of his or her baptism, and that ministry takes place in all aspects of daily life, not just within the walls of the church. Our *Book of Discipline* describes our mission to proclaim the gospel and to welcome people into the body of Christ, to lead people to a commitment to God through Jesus Christ, to nurture them in Christian living by various means of grace, and to send them into the world as agents of Jesus Christ (¶121). Thus, through you—and many other Christians—this very relational mission continues. (The *Discipline* explains the ministry of all Christians and the essence of servant ministry and leadership in ¶¶125–137.)

Essential Leadership Functions

Five functions of leadership are essential to strengthen and support the ministry of the church: identifying and supporting leaders as spiritual leaders, discovering current reality, naming shared vision, developing action plans, and monitoring the journey. This Guideline will help you identify these elements and set a course for ministry.

Lead in the Spirit

Each leader is a spiritual leader and has the opportunity to model spiritual maturity and discipline. John Wesley referred to the disciplines that cultivate a relationship with God as the "means of grace" and suggested several means: prayer, Bible study, fasting, public and private worship, Christian conversation, and acts of mercy. Local church leaders are strongly encouraged to identify their own spiritual practices, cultivate new ones as they grow in their own faith, and model and encourage these practices among their ministry team participants.

Discover Current Reality

"The way things are" is your current reality. How you organize, who does what, how bills get paid and plans get made are all building blocks of your current reality. Spend time with people who have been in this ministry and with your committee members to assess their view of how things are. Use "Christian conversation," one of the means of grace, not only to talk to others openly about their understanding of current reality but also to listen for the voice of God regarding your area of ministry.

Name Shared Vision

"The way things are" is only a prelude to "the way you want things to be." When the church is truly of God, it is the way God would envision it to be. Spend time with your committee and with other leaders in the church to discern the best and most faithful future you can imagine. How can you together identify your role and place in a faithful community that extends itself in its fourfold mission of reaching out and receiving people in the name of God, relating people to God, nurturing them in Christ and Christian living, and sending them forth as ministers into the world? Examine your committee's role and its place in that big picture and try to see yourselves as God's agents of grace and love.

Develop Action Plans

How do you get from here (your current reality) to there (your shared vision)? As a leader, one of your tasks is to hold in view both what is and what is hoped for so that you can build bridges to the future. These bridges are the interim goals and the action plans needed to accomplish the goals that will make your vision a reality. Remember that God may open up many (or different) avenues to that future, so be flexible and open to setting new goals and accepting new challenges. Action plans that describe how to meet interim goals should be specific, measurable, and attainable. While it is faithful to allow for the wondrous work of God in setting out bold plans, balance that boldness with realism. You and your committee will find information and tips here on developing and implementing the shared vision, the goals toward that vision, and the specific action plans that will accomplish the goals.

Monitor the Journey

A fifth responsibility of leaders is to keep an eye on how things are going. Setbacks will surely occur, but effective leaders keep moving toward their envisioned future. Not only will you monitor the progress of your committee's action plans to a faithful future but you will also be called to evaluate them in light of the ministry of the rest of the church. Immerse yourself and your plans in God's love and care. Voices from the congregation (both pro and con) may be the nudging of God to shift direction, rethink or plan, or move ahead boldly and without fear. Faithful leaders are attentive to the discernment of the congregation and to the heart of God in fulfilling the mission of the church.

Welcome to Children's Ministries

Welcome to the world of ministry for, with, and by children.

> *The smiles of children making new discoveries,*
> *the energy of children in a group setting,*
> *the sounds of children in song and in learning, and*
> *the insights of children as God is present in their lives,*
> *all make for a fascinating ministry.*

Remember your own childhood? Think of your first memories of the church. Was it a friendly place? Were you loved? Can you recall special persons or times at church? Where did you learn the stories of God and Jesus? If you didn't attend church as a child, what memories do you want to provide for children?

Think of your church today. Are children welcomed, loved, and cared for in safe surroundings? Are families encouraged, taught, and supported? Is there intentional outreach to children in the surrounding community? Are new children integrated into the life of the church in consistent, caring ways?

Children's Ministries was prepared to enable you as a leader of children's ministries in your congregation. Regardless of your church's size or structure, this Guideline is designed to help you focus on The United Methodist Church's commitment to ministry for, with, and by children. This Guideline contains ideas and suggestions to help you create a church where children experience God's love, feel included in the life of the congregation, and have opportunities to grow in their faith.

You are invited to discover the best design, the most caring persons, the best resources and materials, and the most fruitful programming for children's ministry so that children will flourish and grow in the light of God's love within the environment of your congregation. You are invited to ensure that your congregation particularly includes children in a holistic ministry aimed toward making disciples of Jesus Christ.

Ministry for, with, and by children is an opportunity to work and grow in a variety of arenas. You are not expected to attempt this task alone. You are part of a team with:

- parents, grandparents, caregivers
- the pastor and church staff
- persons in your congregation who are concerned for children
- persons within the connectional United Methodist Church
- persons in the community who care about children.

A Biblical Foundation

Jesus loved children. Who has not heard the beloved story of young Jesus in the Temple speaking with the religious authorities (Luke 2:41-52) or seen at least one picture of the adult Jesus surrounded by and caring for children (based, for example, on Matthew 18:2-5)? In Jesus' culture, as well as ours, children matter. Hebrew parents had an obligation to teach their children the Law and to bring them up to be responsible members of the community—which was also the community of faith.

Jesus would have been familiar with the Deuteronomic commands to teach the faith story to their children. These commands include, "Assemble the people before me [God] to hear my words so that they may learn to revere me as long as they live in the land and may teach them to their children" (4:10) or "When your children ask you in time to come, 'What is the meaning of the decrees and statutes and the ordinances that the LORD our God has commanded you?' then you shall say to your children" the proper recitation of God's mighty acts in history (6:20-25). These injunctions are no less important today.

Children are our treasure, and we must take care of them. In a stinging parable (Matthew 7:9-11), Jesus reminds his hearers that even though we are sinful and make mistakes, we still tend to our children—and God, our parent, tends graciously to us. Children model the pureness of heart and joy inherent in the kingdom of God (Mark 10:13-16). They show us the way.

You are blessed with the most important resources for this ministry—your love for children and your commitment to care for children. With a continual prayer in your heart and God's ever present grace, your ministry will be a blessing to the children and families of your congregation and community. Now go forth, in the name of Jesus, to make a difference. Amen.

Getting Started

What Is My Job?

You are a key person in the children's ministries of your congregation. Your job, as a coordinator of children's ministries in your congregation, assures that children's faith is taken seriously in the life of your church. *Your primary task* (like that of the whole church) *is to help children on their journey as disciples of Jesus Christ.* Given that, what are the relationships and responsibilities for which you are accountable?

Children, and those persons who teach and care for them, are your primary responsibility. Model the love and care that Jesus manifested in his life in order to help children understand their role as disciples. Children are special persons of dignity and worth. Listen to their stories. Know them and call them by name. Keep them safe. Be an advocate for them. They are a valuable part of the congregation, with gifts and blessings to share. In all your actions and reactions, model God's unconditional love for children.

Develop positive relationships with the children and their teachers and with other persons in the congregation. Your role as an advocate for the children will require you to have good working relationships with other congregational leaders and with a variety of other groups. In addition, having a good relationship with parents and knowing the environment or situation in which the children live will add a valuable dimension to your ministry.

Interpret and plan for the spiritual, mental, physical, emotional, social, and moral growth of children. This Guideline will help you respond to children's needs as you plan for activities and programs.

Basic Responsibilities

The responsibilities of your position as coordinator of children's ministries will vary depending on the size and staffing of your church. *If you are in a church with few children,* you are probably the primary person responsible for seeing that the needs of children and youth are met. *If you are in a church with many children and youth,* you may be one of several age-level coordinators. *If there is a paid staff person responsible for children's ministry,* your job may be modified in relation to the staff person's duties.

Whatever the staffing or size of your church, you are responsible for meeting with the church council representing and advocating for children across the entire spectrum of your church's ministries. You have the responsibility of influencing policy and program decisions with the needs of the children in mind, keeping council members informed about the needs of children and the part they play in the life of the church. (There may also be other groups in your congregation's organizational system with whom you will meet, such as the nurture committee, education work area, or children's council.) Whatever the organizational structure of your particular congregation, it is your responsibility to:

- study the needs of children.
- stay in touch with others who care about children. They will help you design and implement programs, initiate ministries, and plan a calendar to best meet the needs of the children and the total church.
- keep in close communication with the children, their parents, and their teachers. This will help you understand the needs, wants, gifts, and graces of the children in your church. Share this information with the church council and the children's council as well as with the total congregation.
- pray intentionally for the children and their families.
- suggest experiences that may be new or innovative.
- advocate for the children. Be strong in your intent that children become a visible and viable part of the church family.
- be realistic in your requests. Being innovative means seeing what the possibilities are and being aware of and in tune with realistic expectations and abilities.
- speak up for quality leadership. Work with the persons who invite teachers and children's workers to help find the best persons for the job.
- speak up for adequate funding. Make sure your financial planners are aware of the needs of all ministries with children. Safe, clean rooms and equipment are expected. Materials to run a program are as necessary as hymnals and bulletins. Assure training opportunities for teachers and leaders.
- do everything possible to ensure that your church is a safe place for children and for the adults who work with them. *Safe Sanctuaries* (see Resources) will help you in this task.
- know about the curriculum materials and other resources that are available. Discover who the resource persons are in your district or conference and do not hesitate to ask for their assistance. Call Curric-U-Phone (1-800-251-8591) for curriculum-related questions.
- be acquainted with the resource materials available from The United Methodist Church. Magazines such as *Leader in Christian Education Ministries, Children's Teacher,* and *Forecast* (curriculum catalog) are valuable tools to aid in your planning. (See Resources.)
- keep in touch with other leaders in the congregation who work with youth, adults, and families. You can accomplish more as a team than alone.
- network with persons in other churches, if possible.

The Coordinator of Children's Ministries

Your job will be rewarding if you know what you are to do. Look over the following sample job description. With other responsible persons (for example, the pastor, the director of Christian education, and the chair of the nurture committee), personalize and date your job description based on your congregation, the setting, and your special gifts. A written job description is helpful whether you are a volunteer or a paid staff person.

Sample Job Description: Coordinator of Children's Ministries
Date Prepared:_____
General Responsibilities
- Represent and advocate for a ministry by, for, and with children in all aspects of congregational life.
- Be well acquainted with the age-level characteristics and needs of children in general and specifically in your neighborhood.
- Coordinate the ministry with children for your congregation.

Specific Responsibilities
- Guide the work of the children's council (if such a council exists).
- Evaluate and assess the present children's ministry program.
- Suggest and implement new possibilities for including children in ministry.
- Work with others, such as the pastor and trustees, to ensure that your church is a safe place for the children and the adults who work with and care for them.
- Serve as a member of the church council, charge or church conference, and other appropriate groups as an advocate for children.
- Recruit persons willing and gifted to serve in the area of children's ministry.
- Offer regular training opportunities for volunteers.
- Know available resources for children and for leaders and teachers who care for children.

Characteristics and Abilities Needed
- Love, care for, and respect children.
- Have faith in God and the ability to share it.
- Have insight and understanding of how children learn and grow.
- Be willing work with others in ministry.
- Be willing to give of yourself and your time.
- Keep an open mind and a willingness to risk and learn!

Training Opportunities
- Read periodicals, such as *Leader in Christian Education Ministries, Children's Teacher, Forecast, Interpreter*, and new materials in the field of children's ministry.

- Contact the appropriate annual conference and district staff to introduce yourself and communicate your congregation's needs for training; request new videos, books, and other resources from the conference center.
- Participate in continuing education in district, conference, or ecumenical settings.
- Network with other area Christian educators and advocates of children.
- Attend FOCUS '05 or '09, a national United Methodist Conference for workers with children.
- Find or start a support group of children's coordinators in the area.

Accountability: Report or Relate to
- the pastor or church staff related to children's ministry
- the church council
- the nurture committee/ work area on education
- the staff/pastor-parish relations committee.

Term of Position: One year; may be renewed or renegotiated.

Time Requirements
- Be in attendance or available for Sunday mornings and weekday programming times.
- Communicate regularly with administrative groups.
- Communicate with teachers and parents regularly.
- Allow ample planning and study time.

Quick-Start Tips

Make an appointment with the staff person responsible for ministry with children (the pastor or director of Christian education). Keep in close communication with that person throughout your tenure.

Study the ministry or mission statement of your congregation, if available. Use this as your guideline for evaluating current programs and developing new programs in children's ministry.

Gather other persons who also care about children. This may be an existing children's council.

Chair and guide the work of the council on children's ministries and your congregation's group of persons responsible for ministry with children.

Formulate your ideas into a yearly plan for ministry with children.

Report on the concerns of children and the plans for ministry to, with, for, and by children to the church council (or its counterpart).

Show appreciation for volunteers who give their time, energy, and abilities for the children.

Additional Hints (for the sake of your health and sanity)
1. **You are only one person, so do not take on more responsibilities than you can handle.** You may want a specific program so strongly that you agree to organize, lead, clean up, and report back to the church. However, if you do it all yourself then *(a)* others are not given the opportunity to be in ministry with children and *(b)* you will eventually suffer from burnout.
2. **Know what your pastor, other staff, and church leaders expect of you.** If what they expect and what you expect are different, talk now! If the job is not defined, then there is no way you can do it. Define the job before you begin; adjust it as you identify new opportunities.
3. **Celebrate each project as it is completed.** Having a list of "to dos" for the year and marking them off as they are completed will give you a sense of a job well done.
4. **Document and evaluate your activities**—both successes and near-successes.
5. **Discover persons with a passion for children's ministries** who you can begin to train to share or take over your job in the future.
6. **Take time off.** Don't become indispensable.

Keeping Our Commitments to Children

The United Methodist Church

The primary task of The United Methodist Church is to *make faithful disciples of Jesus Christ*, including children. You, too, are the church. Your primary task as coordinator of children's ministries is to help the children in your congregation and community to be faithful disciples of Jesus Christ. That should be the foundation on which everything you do is built.

Paragraph 256.1 of the *Discipline* states that in each local church there shall be a church school for the purpose of accomplishing the church's educational ministry. *It is not an option.* There is a continuing need to educate children. You were elected to serve as the leader in children's ministry for your congregation for a term of one year. You are called upon to fulfill the task set out in the *Discipline*. Keep in mind both what is said specifically about the coordinator and also what is included about Christian education, since both help to formulate comprehensive ministries with children.

In addition to the *Book of Discipline, The Book of Resolutions* is an official document of The United Methodist Church. Three resolutions are specifically of benefit to persons active in children's ministries: "Children and Families," "Reducing the Risk of Child Sexual Abuse in the Church," and "Childcare and the Church." Your pastor, church library, or district library may have a reference copy you can borrow to become familiar with these resolutions.

For two quadrennia (1996–2004), the Council of Bishops made children a priority in their own ministries through the **Bishops' Initiative: Children and Poverty**. Bishops led their annual conferences in considering children and the poor (which includes just less than half of the children in the United States) with Bible studies, special initiatives for congregations, accountability at charge conferences, and a variety of programs such as "A Church for All God's Children." The emphasis on children and poverty continues. There is a study guide now available for congregations, "Community with Children and the Poor" (see Resources).

The general boards and agencies of The United Methodist Church take seriously the role of children in the congregation. The General Board of Discipleship, through the Office of Children's Ministries, provides resources for you and others working with children in local congregations. This includes national training events like FOCUS (a quadrennial conference for workers with children planned for 2005 and 2009). This board also carries responsibility through the Curriculum Resource Committee, working with The United Methodist Publishing House, for developing the curriculum component for children. The General Board of Global Ministries advocates for children worldwide and supports United Methodist Women in their "Campaign for Children." The General Board of Church and Society advocates for children in legislative issues. The Commission on United Methodist Men supports the office of Civic Youth Agencies/Scouting. Each of these boards employs staff persons whose major concerns are for children. The General Commission on Finance and Administration provides support for congregations in matters of risk and in keeping children safe. Addresses and web sites are available in Resources or by contacting your pastor.

Your annual conference has persons concerned with children's ministries as well. Generally, conferences have a children's council, a coordinator of children's ministries, or a conference staff person responsible for children's ministries. Districts also may have persons in complementary positions. These persons can help you know about district and conference programs and support for those who work with children. In addition, some conferences have a chapter of Christian Educators Fellowship, whose members will share their knowledge and skills in ministry with children. You may wish to consider joining CEF (see Resources). Contact your conference office for information. Check with your church office or your pastor for the address and telephone number.

Your Commitment

As a young newlywed having recently moved to a new community, I visited the local United Methodist Church. Within a few Sundays, I was invited to join the choir and later to help for one Sunday in the third- and fourth-grade Sunday school class. It wasn't long before I was teaching in vacation Bible school and Sunday school. I fell in love with helping children learn about God's love. That was more than thirty years ago, and I still have that same sensation of pure pleasure when working with children and, now, with adults who work with children. God draws me continually to new places, always with children as the focus. The blessings are many! With pencil and paper handy, please respond to the following as a way to help you prepare for your ministry.

What is your story? What circumstances brought you into children's ministry? Whom did God place in your life to encourage you? What event was the catalyst? Write your own story of how you came to this place of leadership in children's ministry. Tell why!

What special abilities and gifts has God given you? Some are teachers. Some are motivators. Some have gifts of planning or recruiting or visioning or creative problem solving or making terrific bulletin boards or instilling trust, or. ... What gifts has God given to you? List here the gifts you bring. After you have made your list, you may want to ask others what gifts they recognize in you that you may not have yet identified.

At different times in our lives, God speaks to us and leads us in new directions. At this time in your life, God has led you to be a blessing to children, to provide a foundation for their faith development, and to make the church a caring place to grow in God's love. *What is God saying to you now? What is your role at this time and in this place?*

How will your prayer life help you? Regardless of any other spiritual gift or Christian practice, be sure to support yourself and the children in your care with prayer. Even if a prayer is not answered in the way or time frame you desire, the act of prayer itself keeps your concern and your relationships with God and the children in the forefront of your mind and heart. For starters, use the prayer below or write your own.

A Prayer for You
(Hint: This prayer may be used with the children's council by substituting plural pronouns for the singular.)

Almighty God, be with me. I come with a willing heart and many gifts to provide a safe and caring place in the church so that all children will grow in knowledge of you, commitment to Jesus Christ, and love for their neighbor. I ask that you grant the wisdom and vision necessary for the foundation of faith to undergird the children of this congregation. You sent Christ as the example of unconditional love. You sent the Holy Spirit to sustain us in times of difficulty and joy. Send me now to be a strong voice for children. Be with me so that the children of this congregation and community will know your kingdom. In Christ's name, I pray. Amen.

The Congregation's Commitment

In United Methodist churches, parents bring infants and very young children to be baptized. Parents speak on behalf of their children and promise to raise them in the Christian life. The congregation makes a commitment to order their own lives "after the example of Christ, that *this child*, surrounded by steadfast love, may be established in the faith, and confirmed and strengthened in the way that leads to life eternal" (*The United Methodist Hymnal,* Baptismal Covenant II, page 44).

Children become a part of the church family and experience ministry in a variety of ways at an early age. Prayer in the home, at meals, or bedtime helps nurture them in the faith. They come to church and begin to experience the church as a "special place." They begin to interact with each other and learn about treating others with love and respect. As they grow older and become involved in ministry themselves, they begin to live out the promises made by their parents and the congregation at their baptism.

The ministry of Christian education is an all-encompassing task. In its broadest sense, it deals with every aspect of our lives. The Christian faith is communicated to children in essentially two places: the church and the family. It is the primary task of the church to transform persons into disciples. We help children grow in their faith in ways that are appropriate for their age level. They learn in many ways about how God is present in their lives. They participate in the life of the church through Sunday school, weekday settings, corporate worship, and acts of mission and service. At home, children see faith modeled by their parents, and they learn firsthand how to live as disciples.

> Think about your congregation. What are the ways your congregation supports children and their families on their faith journey? What are your congregation's traditions for children's ministry? What vision does your congregation have for children's ministries? How are stories of the faith shared? What opportunities are available for children to express their faith through acts of service and leadership? How are parents sustained in the support of their children's Christian growth in the home? How are families supported in living out their faith when not at church? How are children helped to cope and heal after experiencing a crisis?

On a separate sheet of paper, develop a form similar to the one on page 17. Elicit help from other persons to complete it. This will help form a basis for your ministry with children.

Children's Ministry Profile

Events/Programs Ministries in which Children Participate	Age of Persons Involved	Who Is Responsible? (Person and/or Group)	Budget Information, or How Does Funding Occur?	Values for Children	Values for Families	Values for Our Congregation
Sample: Vacation Bible School	3-yr.-olds through 8th grades and their parents, child care for younger children	Education Committee + Lue, Kim, & Maria, VBS co-directors	Budget line items for Supplies, Equipment, Curriculum, etc. Special donations are requested. No limit.	Stories of faith. Mission education. Fellowship. Leading in worship. Fun. Shared experiences with parents. Developing relationships with others.	Learning together about Jesus in a relaxed, fun setting, creating memories for years to come.	Opportunities for many adults to share faith with children. Outreach to community. Responding to needs for family involvement. Developing relationships with others.

Children's Ministries

What Is Your Role in Keeping Children Safe?

Sadly, the safety of children in the church and at church-sponsored events is no longer something to be taken for granted, as the tragic news from various religious settings has confirmed in recent years. *It is absolutely essential that the church have adequate, updated policies, procedures, and insurance coverage.*

If your congregation already has a child protection policy and procedures, then your role is assessment and advocacy.
- Become familiar with the protection policy and procedures that relate to children.
- Ensure that the policy and procedures are being followed in every dimension of your congregation's ministry with children.
- Take responsibility for yearly updating of procedures.
- Plan for regular communication with the congregation, teachers, and parents regarding the procedures.
- Ask for time at staff meeting and church council to talk about the procedures three or four times a year.
- Assess communication links with new members and new parents (such as the New Member Packet, Welcome to Our Church orientation event, Nursery Home Visitor packet, etc.).

If your congregation has no child protection policy and procedures, then your role is leadership.
- Get and read *Safe Sanctuaries: Reducing the Risk of Child Abuse in the Church,* available from Discipleship Resources (see Resources). This book will help your congregation work step-by-step to make your church a safer place for children and youth and for the adults who work with them.
- Get other people involved, including the pastor, Christian educator, Education/Nurture Committee Chairperson, parents, trustees, and weekday ministry leaders.
- Request the church council to appoint a task force to study the issue and to bring a policy recommendation for formal church approval.
- Follow the steps outlined in *Safe Sanctuaries.*
- Call your conference office for support and training.

Children in the Life of the Congregation

At that time the disciples came to Jesus and asked, "Who is the greatest in the kingdom of heaven?" He called a child, whom he put among them, and said, "Truly I tell you, unless you change and become like children, you will never enter the kingdom of heaven. Whoever becomes humble like this child is the greatest in the kingdom of heaven. Whoever welcomes one such child in my name welcomes me.

"If any of you put a stumbling block before one of these little ones who believe in me, it would be better for you if a great millstone were fastened around your neck and you were drowned in the depth of the sea. Woe to the world because of stumbling blocks! Occasions for stumbling are bound to come, but woe to the one by whom the stumbling block comes!" (Matthew 18:1-7).

Jesus was very clear: *Do not put stumbling blocks in the way of children!* Do we do that in the church? That certainly is not our intent, yet, sometimes we do.
- God gave children minds to think, but do we pay attention to their thoughts?
- God gave children bodies to move, but do we expect them to sit quietly in worship and not disturb the adults?
- God gave children a spirit, but do we fail to provide opportunities for them to express what is on their hearts?
- God gave children insight and abilities to care for others, but do we fail to provide opportunities for them to share their gift of caring with others?

In what ways does your church create stumbling blocks? In what ways does your church remove stumbling blocks and create a clear path for children to walk with God?

Gifts Children Bring to the Church

Children have much to bring to the congregation. Children bring:
- a special spontaneity within congregational life that keeps us smiling, demands flexibility, and adds spice to our life together
- the ability to see things as they really are
- total-body worship of God
- freshness in hymn singing, in celebrating God's love

- new understanding of the world as seen through their eyes
- a reminder of our own vows as we witness their baptism
- their own confusion, isolation, discouragement, fears, loneliness, and pain
- a filling of a void for persons who are childless, whose children are grown, or whose grandchildren live far away
- the ability to make us shed tears because of their vulnerability
- an unhesitating faith and absolute acceptance of God's love
- questions that we forget to ask or are afraid to ask, that push us to think about our own theology, and that press us to articulate our beliefs in new ways. (Children keep us honest.)
- an openness to God
- the ability to unlock love with a simple look
- a way to connect us to today's real world
- a challenge to an "old" way, consideration of a "new" way
- pure, unadulterated JOY!

Children are God's unique gift to us. Do we have the awareness to accept and embrace the gift?

The Organizational Structure of the Church

Because of your responsibility with children, you may have membership in a variety of different committees, councils, and task groups. Membership in these groups may seem to demand an overwhelming number of meetings. However, you may not need to be present at every one. Ask your pastor or staff person with whom you relate to help you complete the Congregational Meeting Commitment Worksheet (page 21) in order to know what is expected of you. Remember: *Someone* should represent concerns of children when events are planned or when decisions are made. Your advocacy is important! Even in a very small congregation, it is important to have an advocate for children. That is you! Fulfill your role with wisdom and caring.

You may be asked (or expected) to participate in:

- the church council—the policy-making and decision-making body for the church
- the nurture committee or education committee. (In many congregations the education committee relies on the coordinator of children's ministries to help plan for the needs of children.) It is also important to have persons on the Outreach and Witness committees who have a heart for children.
- the council on children's ministries, which is responsible under the leadership of the coordinator of children's ministries (that may be you) for planning and overseeing the entire plan for ministry with children. (Although this is optional, it is particularly important and helpful. Information about organizing a council on children's ministries can be found on page 23 of this Guideline.)
- the weekday ministries board. (In many congregations the coordinator of children's ministries may serve on the board of the weekday ministries program.)

Congregational Meeting Commitment Worksheet

Name of Group	Yes, I attend	No, I do not attend	Meeting Schedule	Written Reports	Oral Reports	My Leadership Role
Church Council						
Council on Children's Ministries						
Work Area on Education/Nurture Committee						
Weekday Ministries Board						
Other						

How to Form a Council on Children's Ministries

Depending on the size of your church and the number of children you serve, there may be a need for a Children's Council. Consider forming such a council if your church has *any* of the following characteristics:

- a desire to create a shared ministry with parents, teachers, and congregation
- a large number of children
- two or more classes for each age level (pre-school and elementary)
- many weekday activities
- full-day child care or after-school care for school-age children
- many teachers.

A children's council may help to:
- study the needs of children
- ensure the safety of children involved in the congregation's ministries
- think through possible ministries with children
- talk and work with children and parents or other interested adults
- advise about needed programs for children
- serve as the planning and implementing team for special children's projects and programs
- identify those with gifts for working with children and invite them to serve
- address the needs of special children
- write, revise, implement, and track policies that influence children's ministries.

The membership of the children's council, except for ex officio members, shall be selected by the committee on lay leadership and may include: representative teachers and leaders of children's activities of the church (including its activities in music and the other arts); representative parents; and representatives of work areas or committees (outreach, education, evangelism, missions, stewardship, and worship) related to the church's ministry with children. Ex officio members may include appropriate staff, the chairperson of the education or nurture committees, and the director of the weekday preschool or day care center when the local church sponsors the nursery school or day care center.

Ministry for, with, and by Children

Begin looking for opportunities for children's ministry by checking the worksheet on page 17. Study it, evaluating the variety of opportunities available for children in your congregation. *What is missing? What needs to be strengthened? What needs to change in content or format?* Look at how your congregation reaches out to receive all children, helps children relate their lives to God through Jesus Christ, helps children grow in Christian faith and sends the children into their world to do God's work. Then ask, Do children have opportunities to:

- practice spiritual habits, such as prayer, worship attendance, and service to others
- learn and experience the biblical stories and music of the faith
- share their faith stories
- meet faith "saints" (people with a mature faith who are good examples for children and adults alike) in your own congregation
- experience Scripture at an appropriate developmental level
- learn "rituals" of the faith, such as "Jesus Loves Me," the Lord's Prayer, grace at mealtime, and the Doxology
- experience positive fellowship with other Christians—adults, youth, and children
- experience God's loving care through their teachers and group leaders
- experience opportunities to grow spiritually, physically, socially, psychologically, and emotionally in ways that are appropriate for their developmental level
- contribute to the life of the congregation
- be involved in mission education and stewardship education?

Following is a checklist prepared to show you possible patterns of children's ministry. *No congregation is expected to have every program imaginable.* **Every congregation is expected** to meet the faith needs of the children. Use this list as a way to begin thinking about possibilities and standards for your congregation's ministry with children.

Develop your own list that fits the needs and the setting of your congregation. Think holistically. *Remember, the primary task is to help children to know God and to become faithful disciples of Jesus Christ.* This goal should undergird every option and should be the focus of every intersection of a child's life with the life of the congregation. Only *your congregation* knows the needs and possibilities of *your* setting.

Opportunities for Children

A. Infants, toddlers, and twos are offered:
____ 1. love and acceptance as children of God
____ 2. clean rooms
____ 3. safe rooms
____ 4. clean and safe equipment, furniture, and toys
____ 5. trained, caring teachers
____ 6. Sunday school classes
____ 7. childcare when their parents are involved in church programs
____ 8. a Nursery Home Visitor who connects with them and their parents regularly
____ 9. daycare throughout the week and/or Parent's Day or Morning Out programs
____10. food, clothing, and shelter as needed
____11. a welcome place in worship, fellowship events, and other events where the church family comes together
____12. the opportunity for continuing and dynamic faith development.

B. Preschool Children (ages 3, 4, and 5) are offered:
____ 1. love and acceptance as children of God
____ 2. safe rooms that fit their size, interests, and abilities
____ 3. opportunities for continuing and dynamic faith development
____ 4. Sunday school classes and other discipleship learning opportunities
____ 5. Vacation Bible School classes
____ 6. music experiences through Sunday school and/or a children's choir
____ 7. opportunities to be involved in the stewardship program of the church
____ 8. trained, caring teachers
____ 9. adult friends with whom they feel comfortable
____10. mission studies and opportunities for involvement in mission projects
____11. food, clothing, or shelter as needed
____12. encouragement and support when they bring friends with them to church
____13. weekday classes, such as, preschool, daycare, play groups, nursery school
____14. inclusion in corporate worship services of the congregation
____15. quality child care when their parents are involved in church programs
____16. fellowship times at the church
____17. games, music, and creative activities.

C. Children in the elementary grades are offered:
____ 1. love and acceptance as children of God
____ 2. safe rooms that fit their size, interest, and abilities
____ 3. opportunities for continuing and dynamic faith development
____ 4. Sunday school classes and other discipleship learning opportunities
____ 5. trained, caring teachers
____ 6. adult friends with whom they feel comfortable

____ 7. mission studies and opportunities for involvement in mission projects and justice issues
____ 8. opportunity for stewardship activities and projects
____ 9. vacation Bible school and/or special summer programs
____10. after-school care while parents are still at work
____11. fellowship experiences
____12. choir and other music opportunities
____13. Girl and Boy Scout programs, Camp Fire, 4-H groups
____14. acolyte programs
____15. opportunities to serve in worship through litanies, prayers, Scripture reading, and ushering
____16. concurrent, appropriate programs when parents are involved in adult church programs
____17. food, clothing, or shelter as needed
____18. encouragement to bring friends to church activities
____19. support groups for special concerns such as, divorce of parents, death or other significant loss, and serious illness of sibling
____20. opportunities for intergenerational relationships.

D. Parents of children are offered:
____ 1. opportunities for continuing and dynamic faith development
____ 2. parenting classes
____ 3. Sunday school classes of interest to them
____ 4. food, clothing, shelter as needed
____ 5. assurance of a safe place for their children
____ 6. support groups for special concerns such as loss of a child or spouse, child abuse, and dependence on alcohol or other drugs
____ 7. support from the pastor, professional educator, and other church staff
____ 8. opportunities to learn about baptism and Communion
____ 9. knowledge of what their children are studying
____10. opportunities to teach or lead children's groups
____11. resources for better understanding the ways children grow and what children need
____12. knowledge of what is happening in the community that affects children and the role of the church in the community
____13. knowledge about opportunities to act in support of children in their own communities and throughout the world.

Ministry in the Community and the World

Children can and should take an active part in mission and stewardship activities in their church, community, and world.

Children, especially middle and older elementary children, are interested in and aware of the needs of others. This is a wonderful time to expand their horizons beyond the local church to the community and world around them. They also have an interest in fairness. Combine these two age-level characteristics and you have fertile ground for an extended ministry in several areas. *Sprouts* (see Resources) is an excellent source of ways to help children develop habits of spirituality and action.

Mission and Stewardship
The development of good habits of giving and mission work can't wait until children are adults. Introduce children to mission and stewardship issues. Offer a variety of experiences and opportunities for children (and for the whole congregation) that provide information as well as possibilities to practice giving for others.

Each year the General Board of Discipleship makes available program packets for "The United Methodist Children's Fund for Christian Mission." These packets are free to your church. They describe specific children's mission projects in the United States and around the world. Children are invited to undertake projects in which they learn more about children in specific locations and about mission in general.

All children can become aware of the needs of their communities and the world through such projects as UNICEF, CROP walks, and Heifer Project International. Hold events such as mission fairs, mission Sundays, special project Sundays, and mission summer camp. Select a kit (school, health, sewing, cleaning, layette) for children to build for UMCOR. Set aside some time for children to experience the mission study of a country while United Methodist Women are involved in the study. Consider "Hope for the Children of Africa" as a special mission project.

Include children in stewardship education events and in church-wide stewardship projects. There are many age-appropriate ways for children to understand the stewardship of prayers, presence, gifts, and service. "Stewardship Nuggets" (www.gbod.org/stewardship/articles) helps parents guide children toward a faith-grounded relationship with money, giving, and stewardship.

There are agencies both within the local community and within The United Methodist Church that can help you plan projects and provide information to increase awareness of mission arenas. Contact the persons in your church, district, or conference who serve in the areas of mission and stewardship. Ask for help and information about the possibilities for including children in the extended mission of your church.

Camping

Every conference provides a variety of camping opportunities for children. Church camps provide age-appropriate faith experiences that frequently lead to a life-changing commitment to God. They also provide a place to bond with other United Methodist children and to pursue special interest areas. Other camping opportunities are available through your congregation's participation in Girl Scouts, Boy Scouts, Camp Fire, and 4-H programs. Lifelong friendships often begin in children's camping experiences. In these settings, children are nurtured in a totally different environment. Provide publicity well in advance, as well as funds and transportation for children to attend conference church camp.

Reaching Out to the Community

Invite children from the community to your existing programs and ministries. Also, check your church community and discover some of the needs of children. Is your church located in an area where an after-school program is needed? Perhaps daycare or ill-child care for working parents might be a blessing to your community. What about a tutoring program to meet the educational needs of children? Are there children who are hungry or in need of clothing? You, as coordinator of children's ministries, have a multitude of opportunities to expand the ministries of your church to meet the needs of local children. You can help to create a winning situation for everyone. The neighborhood elementary school(s) will be helpful in an identification process.

Inclusiveness and Ecumenical Awareness

Jesus said, "Go forth into all the world." That commission is not limited to those who are in our country, or look like us, or speak the same language, or celebrate like we do. There are many opportunities for children to learn about others who are different from themselves—whether it is in terms of race, ethnicity, economics, physical or mental ability, or religious beliefs. Be deliberate about providing opportunities for children to learn about and to appreciate others. Provide anti-bias training for adults who work with children. Make discoveries about other religious programs; share ideas, and learn from and about each other. You might invite children from a synagogue or mosque to share their traditions and beliefs (after appropriate preparation for all concerned). World Communion Sunday (the first Sunday of October) is a natural time to learn about other Christian denominations around the world. Join with other congregations near you in a neighborhood vacation Bible school, Thanksgiving program, or Children's Sabbath observance.

Bishops' Initiative: Children and Poverty
In the previous two quadrennia children, as part of The United Methodist Church, are called to join the Bishops' Initiative on Children and Poverty. As a part of this emphasis, we are called to help children who are in need. Look at the needs of children in your community. Look at the needs of children globally. Consider using the "Community with Children and the Poor" study guide, "United Methodist Children's Fund for Christian Mission," "A Church for All God's Children," and "Hope for the Children of Africa" as a part of your year's programming. Be alert to opportunities that help children and their families grow in awareness of the needs of others in their communities.

Children's Sabbath
Each year on the third weekend in October, people of faith gather in churches, synagogues, temples, and other houses of faith to lift up the needs of children. Become a part of this special weekend of learning, praying, advocacy, and worship. Contact the Children's Defense Fund (see Resources) for a Children's Sabbath planning guide. Invite other congregations and faiths to join the planning. If the third weekend of October will not work for your congregation, select another time.

Preserving Creation
The important issues of ecology and environment, centering on stewardship of our Earth home, present excellent arenas in which children may become actively involved. Recycling and area cleanup projects provide fun learning (and productive) experiences for children of all ages. These can be organized with adult groups in your congregation, as a fellowship group or after-school program, or with a Sprouts program.

Organize and Plan for the Year

Check and double-check your plans to ensure a smooth-running program. Some churches provide programming the year round; others, from September through June. *No matter what pattern your church follows, a year-long planning calendar is a must.*

Find out where your complete church calendar is kept, who records information, and how to schedule the events for which you are responsible. Note those events already on the church calendar that include or affect children's ministries. It is also helpful to be aware of community events. Get a calendar like The United Methodist Program Calendar (see Resources), which includes planning suggestions. Begin with those dates already set on your church calendar. List upcoming dates of events planned for children and coordinate programming with other church ministries to avoid conflicts. Meet regularly with staff to look ahead at upcoming events.

List meetings and events that are already set. Block time for preparation and for quality programming. Add to these activities the dates for ordering curriculum: July, October, January, April. Also, note dates for purchasing attendance books and supplies. Call your conference and district offices to find out dates for teacher training events and church camp experiences. Setting up the calendar is critical to your program ministries.

Now, take a look at what is planned. Are there opportunities to help children grow as disciples and as spiritual beings? Is there a variety of activities for children's varying interests? Are family and intergenerational experiences included? What is missing? Where are potential difficulties? What will take long-term planning or group planning? For additional help in planning, see chapter 3 of *The Ministry of Christian Education and Formation: A Practical Guide for your Congregation* (see Resources).

As the coordinator of children's ministries you are a link in the connectional system of The United Methodist Church. Through you, in cooperation with the work area or committee chairpersons, the resources and experiences of the denomination become available to your local church. Call upon the services and resources of the district and conference coordinators of children's ministries. Pastors and district superintendents can furnish names and addresses of these persons for you. Plan to attend FOCUS, (see page 14). Budget for this in advance. Check with district and conference personnel about upcoming events for workers with children, and see the inside back cover for general agency contacts.

30 Guidelines for Leading Your Congregation

Weekday Ministries

Weekday ministry is possible in any size church. In all churches, the goal and the vision must be that which is best for children. In 2000, General Conference adopted a resolution on "Child Care and the Church." This resolution guides a congregation's ministry through the week with children to assure that quality programs are established and implemented to meet the physical, emotional, spiritual, and mental needs of children today. Jesus said, "Let the little children come to me" (Mark 10:14). He also said, "Whoever welcomes one such child in my name welcomes me" (Matthew 18:5).

Childcare in the church is not a new field. Several thousand of our congregations sponsor weekday programs such as daycare; Parents' Day Out; preschool; after-school care; and respite care for children with handicapping, abusive, or other special conditions. Many of these programs are intentional ministries of the congregations. Some use space rented from a church, and some are integrated holistically as a congregational ministry.

We can fully accept children as Jesus did. We can invite them into our fellowship and nurture them.

What Is Weekday Ministry?

Weekday ministry is *mission* work at its very best. The most important resource of any society is its children. Many children in our communities are in need of safe, quality care during times when parents are at work.

Weekday ministry is Christian education, nurture, and faith development. During the critical early childhood and early elementary years, children form basic attitudes about the world and themselves. In addition, it is during this time that children form trust, the fundamental requirement for faith development. The church best reflects the Christian faith when it supports families at this crucial time and provides an example of the highest, Christlike qualities.

Weekday ministry is stewardship. Rooms that might otherwise be empty throughout the week are used for the education and formation of children.

Weekday ministry is evangelism. Families of young children who have found love and concern for their children in your church's weekday ministry often become part of the church family. Regardless of whether this happens, people are still receiving the good news of God's love through interactions with people of faith.

Weekday ministry is a business requiring dependable income, realistic expense projections, binding agreements, accountability, and liability.

What Weekday Ministry Is Not

It is also important to note what weekday ministry is not.

Weekday ministry is *not* a fundraiser. Everything has a price tag. Depending on the form of your program, participants expect to be charged appropriate tuition and fees, which include the expenses for utilities, supplies, and teachers. Tuition will not affect the tax-exempt status of the church if your church is incorporated and your policy statement shows the relationship of the weekday program to the governing body of the church. Although fees may cover the expenses of the program, quality care is expensive. Your church should not expect to make money from any weekday ministry. Any excess funds should be held in trust for "lean" times in the ministry and for increasing benefits for staff in a field that is generally underpaid.

Weekday ministry is not easy. Weekday ministry means shared space. It means wear and tear on the building, more things to store, and more programs to schedule. Meeting licensing requirements may require installation of smoke detectors or push-bar doors. In regions where it snows, the parking lot has to be plowed on days other than Sunday. Other requirements may include regular testing of the water supply, the fire extinguishers, and the safety of the building to meet health department codes. Meeting the requirements will provide a safer place for all persons for every day of the week. Whether or not there is a weekday ministry, most of these requirements should be in effect for the safety of all persons in your building.

Accountability

All education in a United Methodist church is provided through the nurture or education committees. A weekday ministry board would work with and report to the agency responsible for Christian education in the church. The staff/pastor-parish relations committee might be responsible (with the weekday ministry board) in hiring the director.

Responsibility

A weekday program cannot be taken lightly or casually. It is a sacred trust and a legal and moral responsibility. Once begun, it needs perpetual care and nurturing. The congregation needs to assess its understanding of discipleship as it relates to the weekday ministry program and to reassess and update the program periodically. The Resources section suggests guides for beginning or reevaluating a program.

Weekday Ministry Programs

What Is Weekday Ministry Here?
Regardless of the kinds of weekday ministry offered, the church has the opportunity and the mandate to include children from various socioeconomic, cultural, and racial and ethnic backgrounds. Children learn by example. They first develop faith through trust in the adults around them. Their parents often select church-based weekday programs because they feel they can trust the church to care for their children regardless of their own religious affiliation or background. We must work hard to keep that trust by providing quality learning experiences in a safe environment.

A weekday ministry board may be responsible for governing one or more of the following programs in your church. For assistance in setting up or training a weekday ministry board, see the *Director's Manual for Weekday Ministry* (see Resources).

For Younger Children (infants through kindergarten)
Daycare: A program for infants, toddlers, and pre-elementary children that may begin as early as 7:00 A.M. or earlier and continue as late as 6:00 P.M. or later. It provides care and meals and offers developmentally appropriate activities in a safe atmosphere of love and concern for each child.

Preschool/Nursery School: A half-day program for children two to five years old that provides developmentally sound activities in an atmosphere of love and concern for each child.

Kindergarten: A half- or full-day program for children five years of age that has the added goals of teaching readiness skills to children prior to entrance into first grade.

Parents' Day/Night Out Program: A half-day, all-day, or evening program of care and activities for children while parents are provided free time.

Care for Special Needs Children: A program for children who are recovering from physical or emotional trauma or abuse; for whom English is a second language and who need tutoring; or who have other special needs. Establishing such a program could provide a service that is unavailable in the community.

For Older Children
Before- and After-School Care: A program that provides a safe and enriching atmosphere for school-age children who otherwise would be without

supervision before and after school. The program could be extended to a full-time program during the summer or school holidays. Activities may include faith enrichment fellowship, scouting groups, music, service projects, and academic enrichment.

Fellowship Groups: Meet once a week or less. They provide opportunities for development of "group" within the church.

Telephone Ministry to "Latchkey" Children: A program in which children could call or be called when they are alone at home. It is an excellent way to connect children with caring adults.

For All Children
Ill-Child Care: A specialized ministry for children who have minor illnesses, such as colds or flu. Working parents are especially grateful for this ministry.

Evening/Night Care: Particularly important for parents who work second or third shifts.

Resources

Children's Ministries Resources

- *Campaign for Children*—Phase III Booklet (Service Center # 5573, free 1-800-305-9857). Special emphasis of United Methodist Women.
- *Children's Teacher.* Quarterly magazine. Available with a curriculum order from Cokesbury.
- *Children's Sabbath.* Yearly planning manual available from Children's Defense Fund. (See Additional Helpful Resource Agencies below.)
- *Children Worship!* by MaryJane Pierce Norton (Nashville: Discipleship Resources, 1997. ISBN 0-88177-223-2). Thirteen-session worship education resource helps congregations incorporate children (ages 5–8) into the worshiping community. Can easily be adapted for parenting classes and intergenerational retreats.
- *Community with Children and the Poor: A Study Guide for Congregations* by Deb Smith (Nashville: Cokesbury, 2003. ISBN X516543). A resource in support of the Bishops Initiative on Children and Poverty, relating beyond local settings to systemic and global issues.
- *The First Three Years: A Guide for Ministry with Infants, Toddlers, and Two-Year-Olds,* by Mary Alice Donovan Gran, editor (Nashville: Discipleship Resources, 1995, 2001. ISBN 0-88177-324-7). A comprehensive manual for the congregation's ministry to young children and their families. Completely reproducible.
- *Foundations: Shaping the Ministry of Christian Education in Your Congregation* (Nashville: Discipleship Resources, 1993. ISBN 0-88177-123-6). Provides a foundation for building a solid Christian education ministry in your congregation.
- *Hand in Hand: Growing Spiritually With Our Children,* by Sue Downing (Nashville: Discipleship Resources, 1998. ISBN 0-88177-224-0). Designed specifically to help parents raise their children as Christian disciples.
- *Helping Children Cope With Divorce,* by Jenni Douglas Duncan (Nashville: Discipleship Resources, 1999. ISBN 0-88177-270-4). Designed to help congregations design and implement a support group for children ages 6-10. Eight sessions with lots of helps included.
- *Making God Real for a New Generation: Ministry With Millennials Born From 1982 to 1999,* by Craig Kennet Miller and MaryJane Pierce Norton (Nashville: Discipleship Resources, 2003. ISBN 0-88177-376-X). A series of articles about the world of the millennials.

- *Leader in Christian Education Ministries.* Quarterly magazine. Available with a curriculum order from Cokesbury.
- *Let There Be Peace in the Classroom,* by Jenni Douglas Duncan (Nashville: Discipleship Resources, 2002. ISBN 0-88177-385-9). A guide for teachers and leaders in Sunday school and other groupings of children. This book tackles the hard issues related to discipline and managing a classroom.
- *The Ministry of Christian Education and Formation: A Practical Guide for Your Congregation,* by the Christian education staff of the General Board of Discipleship (GBOD) (Nashville: Discipleship Resources, 2003. ISBN 0-88177-395-6). A helpful and practical "must have" book for planning Christian education ministries for your congregation.
- *Out of the Basement,* by Diane C. Olson (Nashville: Discipleship Resources, 2001. ISBN 0-88177-351-4). A "must have" resource that provides a vision for holistic ministry, recognizing children as growing disciples of Jesus Christ.
- *Pockets* magazine (Nashville: Upper Room). A devotional magazine with Bible study, games, activities, and stories specifically for school-aged children. Available by individual or group subscription.
- *Putting Children and Their Families First: A Planning Handbook for Congregations,* by Laura Dean Friedrich (New York: GBGM Service Center) (Order #2627). Use to assess needs and develop plans for children and families in their community.
- *Safe Sanctuaries: Reducing the Risk of Child Abuse in the Church,* by Joy Thornburg Melton (Nashville: Discipleship Resources, 1998. ISBN 0-88177-220-8). Outlines policies and procedures to help congregations be safe places for children and youth and for the adults who care for them.
- *Sprouts: Nurturing Children Through Covenant Discipleship,* by Edie Genung Harris and Shirley Ramsey (Nashville: Discipleship Resources, 2002. ISBN 0-88177-389-1). Explains weekly support for children grades 3-6 to live as disciples of Christ.
- *What Every Teacher Needs to Know About . . . ,* by the Christian education staff of the GBOD (Nashville: Discipleship Resources, 2002. ISBN 0-88177-374-3). Series of ten booklets on basic Christian education topics: Teaching, Curriculum, People, Classroom Environment, The United Methodist Church, Theology, Living the Faith, The Bible, Faith Language, and Christian Heritage. Available in sets of ten of any one topic or as a complete set.

From the Office of Children's Ministry

The following four resources are available by download from the web site or by contacting The Office of Children's Ministries at the General Board of Discipleship (www.gbod.org/children); telephone 1-877-899-2780 Ext. 1761.

- *The United Methodist Children's Fund for Christian Mission.* A packet that includes a map and six annual projects for mission education for children.
- "Childcare and the Church," in *The Book of Resolutions, 2004.* The official statement on weekday ministry of the United Methodist Church. (Check also with your pastor.)
- *Faith Development of Children.* A concise look at how children grow and develop. Includes a chart.
- *Information: Children's Ministries* newsletter. Back issues are available.

Mission Projects for Children

- The United Methodist Children's Fund for Christian Mission, P.O. Box 34003, Nashville, TN 37203-0003. Phone 1-877-899-2780 Ext. 1761.
- Heifer Project, International, P.O. Box 727, Little Rock, AR 72203. Phone 888-422-1161.
- Hope for the Children of Africa, UMCOM, P.O. Box 320, Nashville, TN 37203-0320. www.umcgiving.org/content/order. Click on "Hope for the Children of Africa" for interpretation helps.
- School or Health Kits, United Methodist Committee on Relief (UMCOR), UMCOR Depot, 131 Sager Brown Road, P.O. Box 850, Baldwin. LA 70514-0850. Phone 800-814-8765. http://gbgm-umc.org/umcor/kits.cfm.
- UNICEF, 3 United Nations Plaza, New York, NY 10017. Phone 212-326-7000.

Weekday Ministries Resources

- *BibleZoneLive,* a fun, inspirational way to teach the Bible to children. Kits include Teacher's guide and kits available from Cokesbury. Preschool, younger elementary, and older elementary
- *Civic Youth Serving Agencies/Scouting Packet,* available free from Civic Youth Serving/Scouting Office of United Methodist Men. P.O. Box 340006, Nashville, TN 37203-0006; lcoppock@gcumm.org.
- *Director's Manual for Weekday Ministries,* by Barbara Snell McLain (Nashville: Discipleship Resources, 2003. ISBN 0-88177-383-2). Help leaders build a quality weekday ministry and expand existing weekday programs.

• *Just Add Kids.* A series of curriculum pieces for preschool (ages 3-5) and elementary (ages 6-10) for children to be involved as they learn Bible stories. Separate books for stories, games, crafts, and music. Available from Cokesbury.

Resource Agencies

• *Children's Defense Fund.* Advocacy for children. Sponsors Children's Sabbath. Newsletter and other helpful information available about today's children. P.O. Box 90500, Washington, DC 20090-0500. 202-662-3589 or www.childrensdefense.org.

• *Christian Educators Fellowship.* Professional group for persons, both volunteer and employed, who are leading Christian educational ministries in congregations. CEF is a national organization that also has annual conference chapters. Contact Corinne Van Buren, Christian Educators Fellowship Office, P.O. Box 24930, Nashville, TN 37202, 615-749-6870 or www.cefumc.org.

• *National Association for the Education of Young Children (NAEYC).* Accredits high quality early childhood programs. Its membership organization publishes the magazine *Young Children,* as well as books, pamphlets, videos, and posters. Write to NAEYC, 1834 Connecticut Ave., NW Washington DC, 20009. Telephone 1-800-424-2460 for membership information and resource list.

• *School Age Notes: A National Resource Organization on School Age Care.* Excellent newsletter resource for after-school and summertime weekday ministry for school-aged children. P.O. Box 40205, Nashville, TN 37204-0205, 615-242-8464 or www.schoolagenotes.com.

• *Department of Human Services.* Each state sets standards for preschool and school-aged programs. Contact your state office for the licensing standards. Additionally, school principals and counselors, community health personnel, scout leaders, and others are helpful connections in meeting the needs of all children in your community.

General Church Resources

• *The Book of Discipline of The United Methodist Church,* 2004 (Nashville: The United Methodist Publishing House; available from Cokesbury).

• *Guidelines for Leading Your Congregation: 2005–2008* (Nashville: Abingdon Press; available from Cokesbury). Especially appropriate Guidelines: *Christian Education, Small Group Ministries,* and *Scouting and Civic Youth Serving Ministry.*

• *Job Descriptions for Local Church Leaders* (Nashville: Discipleship Resources, 1997, 2001. ISBN 0-88177-344-1). A packet with loose sheets describing the positions of all local church officers and a manual for leadership development which includes training designs.

- *Sharing God's Gifts* (United Methodist Communications, Free, Call 1-888-862-3242) About the structure and organization of The United Methodist Church.
- *Program Calendar* (United Methodist Communications, Free, Call 1-888-862-3242). Available in a variety of formats. Contains various helps for planning for United Methodists congregations.
- *What Every Leader Needs to Know* [Series] (Nashville: Discipleship Resources, 2004).
- Cokesbury Speciality Imprinting Service offers a large selection of high quality products that can be imprinted with your church's name, logo, or other custom copy. Speciality Imprinting is a creative, affordable way for you to promote your church's identity, programs, and activities. Available at your nearest Cokesbury store or call 1-800-237-7511.